lost in the cosmos

a collection of poems by Morgan Rose

Gotham Books

30 N Gould St.
Ste. 20820, Sheridan, WY 82801
https://gothambooksinc.com/

Phone: 1 (307) 464-7800

© 2024 *Morgan Rose*. All rights reserved.

No part of this book may be reproduced, stored in a retrieval system, or transmitted by any means without the written permission of the author.

Published by Gotham Books (October 18, 2024)

ISBN: 979-8-88775-880-0 (P)
ISBN: 979-8-88775-881-7 (E)

Because of the dynamic nature of the Internet, any web addresses or links contained in this book may have changed since publication and may no longer be valid.

The views expressed in this work are solely those of the author and do not necessarily reflect the views of the publisher, and the publisher hereby disclaims any responsibility for them.

Contents

forgotten on the shore 1
i need you 2
last kiss 4
pretty sinkholes 5
last event 6
lodged 7
rowing around 8
on stage 9
instructor 10
ending up with nothing 11
further than the end 12
push and pull 13
lies in good faith 14
hanging on 15
falling 16
love in memories 17
end of war 19
following the moon 20
waiting for you 21
too close 22
i get it now 23
the negative aspects 24
not your jester 26

made to obey	27
cut off	28
hindsight	29
the opposite of empathy	30
affirmations	31
disingenuous	32
break the screen	33
incomplete	34
changes	35
alone in here	36
ending connections	37
i win	38
countdown	39
hopes and wishes	40
i'm me again	41
false image	42
user	43
harmonizing	44
breaking a routine	45
good intentions	46
restart	47
remembering, and that's all	48
trust v. pattern	49
used	50

destructive thoughts 51
love's downfall 52
stuck 53
losing 54
come with me 55
now we really do look the same 56
push it away 57
letting you go 58
it's too different now 59
here for you 60
to be winter... 61
in need of a reset 62
remember me 63
a short lived sight of beauty 64
low battery.. 65
all for you 66
wishing and wanting 67
inside 68
breaking the lines we dance between 69
the sound of stagnancy 70
About the author 71

dedicated to everyone who's helped me get through the times
i've written about

forgotten on the shore
11/01/2018

if left on the beach,
there are only two paths.
to be stolen,
or to drift away.
so please leave me in the sand.

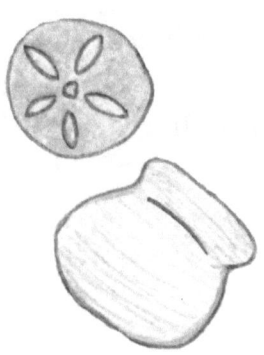

i need you
04/21/2019

i am the deep sea
alone i am dark, cold
unforgiving
i take what you give me
i give nothing in return
a black hole

you are the sun
alone you are hot, mean
scorching all that pass
burning all that you touch
a house ablaze

without the sea
without the sun
nothing would be maintained
together they are unified
bringing and sustaining life

dancing together
they bring about joy
happiness, vitality
a song, a dream
achieving peace

i am your deep sea
giving, caring

loving
i hold your warmth close
i need you

i am your sun
empathetic, kind
warm
i hold your depth close
i need you

last kiss
03/17/2021

true loves kiss with poison tucked under your tongue, come cry at my funeral and say you thought i'd be the one

pretty sinkholes
08/23/2021

leave me in the whirlpool if your help means that you come near it
it'll pull you down too, don't worry
a little algae couldn't be that bad, and i'm the one that swam down here anyways
i must've forgotten that these aren't much more than pretty sinkholes

last event
09/04/2021

picked out an outfit for the funeral
plain jeans, some shoes i always wear
it's nothing special, but it's not like i am either
so it's perfect for the occasion
and i even get to choose the date

lodged
09/07/2021

i was just a pebble lying quiet on the side of the road
you drove by and got me stuck in your tire
and i find myself wishing for the rain for once

rowing around
09/18/2021

i dropped one of my oars in the river a few miles back
at least i think it was a few miles
i can't tell anymore, it's like this scenery is all the same
hard to believe i'm doing anything but going in circles

on stage
09/19/2021

saying i've reached the end of the line would imply that something is over
but it feels more like i've reached the end of the song
the production still goes on, the crew sets up the stage again
i guess i could stay & see what happens next

… did anyone say how long this shows runtime was?

instructor (haiku)
09/19/2021

signed up for a class
this week focused on goodbyes
why'd you grab the chalk?

ending up with nothing
09/21/2021

i'm drowning myself and i'm drowning my past and i'm drowning the memories that couldn't last and everything's trying to break it all down and i wish i could join it 6ft in the ground because everything looks like it's falling apart and i wish i could turn and go back to the start i'd redo it all and try it again and then maybe i'd at least end up with a friend

further than the end
10/25/2021

jumped off the ledge and hit rock bottom
i didn't expect to be able to breathe, and i didn't expect
the ground to be quicksand
there's no light down here, when the sun sets i think
i'll be blind
and i don't think i'll make it til morning
i get why it's so hard to get back out now

push and pull
10/31/2021

plug the drain, let the hot water run
show the sink what it's like to feel full
let the water overflow
let it rain on the tile
close the faucet, pull the plug
this kinda seems like it's fun

lies in good faith
11/03/2021

you told me "we're forever" stood with one foot out the door,
said "you're the one that i adore",
now i'm the one that you ignore.
why'd you treat me like a chore, why don't you call me anymore? why's it different now? this isn't how it was before.
i asked you and you said you'd care, "i'll change!", you looked at me and swore. said "baby please, i'll be nice more", but when you're mad i'm called a whore. yeah, sorry, i can't stay with you. don't call me anymore.
i didn't realize this was something that i'd be the one to pay for, but, you know it best my love, all is fair in love and war

hanging on
11/10/2021

you grabbed my hand when i fell off the edge and i know it would hurt less to let myself hit the ground than to stay and hang around but even so, i dread the day where you decide to let go

falling
11/13/2021

the wind whips past my ears
feeling velocity increase
i can't hear or see a thing
this is where i find the peace

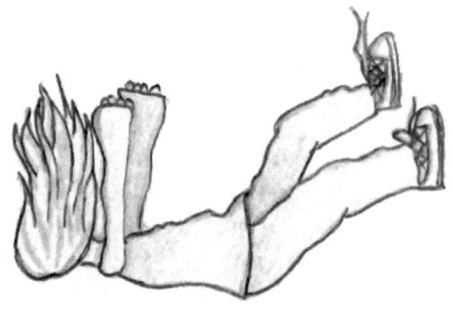

love in memories
11/14/2021

i want to feel love
like when the boy in 7th grade told me his dream was to kiss someone in the rain before he kissed me in the rain
like when i was held so tightly that i felt like if i died in that moment it would be alright
like when i was told that life wouldn't be the same without me in it
like when i was told that i make a difference
like waking up in their arms after going to sleep mad at each other
like sleeping next to each other when you're mad in the first place
like holding their sweater when you can't hold them and feeling their comfort all the same
like when a voice felt like home
like when i talk and it feels like anything i could possibly say is important
like feeling heard
like getting a call just for company even if nobody has anything to say
like falling asleep to the sound of someone talking
like waking up with sunshine shining bright through open curtains and immediately hearing their voice
like walking through nature hand in hand, feeling as though i was where i should be
like the feeling of being where i should be

like when awkward silences are impossible to make
like comfort and familiarity
like the warmth from the sun
i'll wait to feel that again

end of war
11/15/2021

false red flags, white dyed with the blood of those who surrendered but it wasn't enough

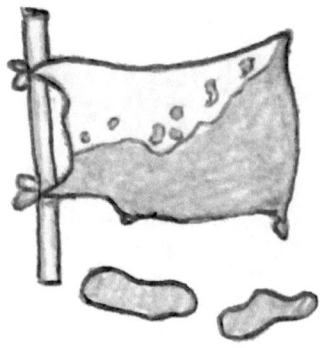

following the moon
11/20/2021

like moths to flames we seek the light which guides us home
it's not your fault that all the streets are lined with lamps
you'll find the highway soon

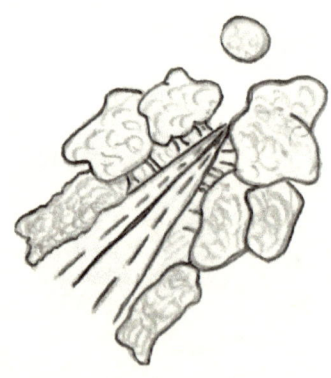

waiting for you
12/19/2021

i'll go to space with you, and i'll stay when you go back down
just tell me when you're headed back, i promise that i'll stay around
i'll be here waiting, and i get it, you can't always be in space
but i'll still be here when you're back, i guess i have some time to waste
'cause even if the cosmos is a lonely place to be,
i'll stay here just for you if i'm the star you like to see

too close
12/22/2021

i would've followed where you led me, i put full trust in you, my heart went further than my sleeve and bled right onto you and yeah i'm sorry that it stains but does it mean you have to go? it does? that's fine i guess, then go. i'll be fine on my own. i was a fool for you but i won't look like one alone

i get it now
12/25/2021

i think i'm done now and it's fine, i'm glad you showed me all the signs i had to see to understand that i could never call you mine 'cause things with us could have been good but you kept me misunderstood so when you realize what you missed and you miss me, know that you should

the negative aspects
12/30/2021

after i'm gone what do i leave behind?
what's gonna be on everybody's mind?
i don't think it looks good, i don't think it comes close,
they'll remember how you always made shit change course,
how you had no commitment and you showed no remorse,
how you gave yourself rules that you couldn't enforce,
how each challenge and change just made you start to choke,
how you treated every single thing like a joke,
and the weird way you spoke, and the dumb shit you said,
how you'd act like your brain is too big for your head
like you know more than them,
like you're better than them,
how you'd act like a jewel in a pile of gems,
and add on all the ways that you hurt all your friends,
which you didn't make any attempts to amend,
and the way that you'd act, how you brought people down,
and how often you made yourself look like a clown,
how you held onto things that you knew would just hurt you,
how you acted in ways that betrayed all your virtues,
how you said you'd be good but it never held up,

and that time you fucked up, and that time you fucked up,
and that time you fucked up and couldn't clean it up,
and they saw that you always make good things go wrong,
and they know that you lied when you said you were strong,
but they've known about all of this stuff all along,
so maybe they'll all just be happy you're gone

not your jester
01/15/2022

if i'm a joke i'll make it funny, if i'm a game i'll make you lose
i'm not your fool, i'm not your dummy
i've got better things to do
i hope you catch me in his DMs, i hope you wish you were in mine
but i don't play games, i don't tell jokes, and i do not waste my time

made to obey
01/23/2022

i love you always and forever, except there's one condition
you're as disposable as money which means i make the decisions
and you're gonna answer to me if i have any suspicions
because i don't think it's right for you to have no supervision
oh, and by the way, you're gonna switch up your ambitions
you're gonna follow where i go, and you can't be my opposition
and if you wanna make a move you're gonna need to ask permission
and you'll do what i say because we're following my vision
and i- what was that?
you said that's more than one condition?
oh yeah i forgot to mention, you don't get any opinions
i thought that i was clear when i said i make the decisions and that there won't be opposition,
i think you need to learn to listen

cut off
01/30/2022

i'm gonna work to cut the strings 'cause i can tell i shouldn't stay but if you wanted me dead and gone then that's all you had to say and i guess that there was tension which i guess i wasn't seeing, i wish you could've just told me that but i guess i'm fine with leaving

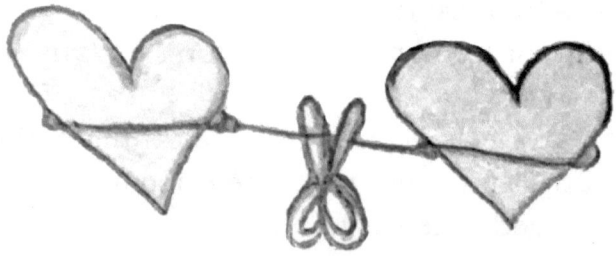

hindsight
02/26/2022

"you're so important to me and i really hope you stay"
you stuffed the note into my pocket and you threw me away
i noticed you wrote down the lies that you told me the other day
i really should've known by then that you don't mean what you say
but how could i know? i thought i found where i was meant to be
i overlooked the flags that were planted in front of me
in the haze of pink and red it got a little hard to see
and i clung onto some things that were never meant for me
but when what's for me wants to go, it's not my choice to make it stay
i don't know where or what went wrong, but i have nothing else to say
so i don't hope for resolution, i won't let the past replay
i'll do my best to look ahead, and hope the past has been okay

the opposite of empathy
03/04/2022

you put me in the guillotine while you screamed "it's inhumane!" as if that's your head on the floor. as if that's you who felt the blade

affirmations
03/08/2022

i will not overstay
i won't drain myself dry
i will end up okay
i don't need to ask why
i will leave when i'm hurt
i won't settle the score
i won't stay through the worst
i will love myself more
i won't stay in the rain
i won't settle for less
i'll be friends with the pain
and let fate solve the rest

disingenuous
03/26/2022

they're not really gonna care unless they're benefitted too,
they'll say "id die for all my friends" until it comes down to you,
they'll show you that it's bad to have you close and it's not something they could do and they'll get good at showing just how much it hurts them to love you.
they'll rip your heart off of your sleeve then say it's you who's being cruel,
they'll leave you wishing that you knew the hoops you'd end up jumping through,
all the problems that you'd see and all the things that you'd see too and that they weren't really there and that nothing they say is true
 and they'll make promises and plans and then they'll let them all fall through
because your time's a waste,
you'll be replaced,
this isn't something new but you know the drill and you know they will,
so here's hoping that you grew

break the screen
03/29/2022

it's all scripted tv and static and the drama's not dramatic i wish that i could change the channel 'cause this programs gone erratic. cut the cable, break the screen, wish i knew how to end the scene, i don't know what this show's about, and i can't tell what it means. i'm just a character on stage- what's my next line? please flip the page, please change the cast, please change the show, i'll dress up fast, i'll change my role, i'll do what's asked i'm sorry... got a bit carried away, i know. i've got a role to play, but one day i'll leave and i'll go back home. i'll be myself again someday, i'm sick of living in a haze of things that don't really feel real with episodes stuck on replay, but i don't think there's much to do i signed my whole life away, put pen to paper, wrote my name and said i'd be here every day. i mean i must've, right? i'd leave this show if i had any say but i feel stuck up on a stage that's taken parts of me away. i'd quit this whole show if i could! and sometimes i feel like i should just get right up and walk right out the doors and go find something good but there's no door, there is no out, there is no exit, you are HERE. you're just an actor, know your role, i know i made all of this clear: you don't exist, there is no You, and all of this is your career. and cast, remember to speak up, make sure the audience can hear. maybe this time you'll give that crowd a good reason to cheer

incomplete
04/04/2022

i'll send you a gift so you can keep a part of me in case i'm just your memory, in case you can't just come see me because i moved away, i thought i should find a different place to stay, i couldn't stay where i was staying, where i stayed was not ok but it's ok 'cause i can say that now, and sorry if i skipped goodbyes and if i left like that, i'm sorry that i didn't tell you why, i'm sorry that my bags are packed, sorry for what my words imply, sorry if i'm not coming back and i'm so sorry that i

changes
05/18/2022

its been feeling cold since about october
my life changed ever since you walked in
i wish that it could have been better than it's been
and i really wish you could've been sober
and i don't know why things had to play out in that way
it sucks right now but i know this won't stay forever
i wish you well but i can't say that whatsoever
i wish you well but i still hope you stay away

alone in here
05/22/2022

got chased towards a dead end room, so i ran in and shut the door
i cant get out, you can't get in, bad things won't happen anymore
yeah solitude is something i'm not sure i can afford
but if i do it this way at least nobody's getting bored

ending connections
06/19/2022

check the thread for me please, has the elastic gone rotten? replace that string, here, tie up these. forget what once has been forgotten. plan a visit to my past and then stuff her ears with cotton and come back with empty buckets to put all those empty thoughts in

i win
06/20/2022

i'll dip my toes in quickly first, i need to test the water first
feels a bit heavier than normal but i can breathe and i'm not hurt
i'm swimming from the shallow end down to the side that's like 6 feet,
told you "i'll race you to the bottom" but i'll admit that i did cheat

countdown
07/12/2022

16 sent texts that say "i love you"
15 drinks in, bottle's dry
14 reasons i should give up
13 reasons i should try
12 things i did wrong this week
11 times i had to cry
10 things i did to make it better
9 times better got denied
8 account passwords updated
7 things given and sold
6 transactions heading out
5 straight days of feeling cold
4 missed calls all with voicemails
3 assignments overdue
2 things telling me to stay
1 thing i still wanted to do, but there's
0 strings attached to keep me tethered to the ground and i think i might float away so if i miss you, see you around

hopes and wishes
07/12/2022

desperately reaching out in desperate despair
like i'm desperate to find what's supposed to be there
and i'm desperate for me to stop feeling so scared
i am desperate but stuck in the loop

i got lost when i stepped a bit off of my route
now i'm lost while in search of finding my way out
and i'm lost putting meaning to what it's about
i am lost, i'm not sure what to do

i'm waiting to stop feeling like i need to run
i'm waiting for these things that might not ever come
and i'm waiting until i can stop feeling dumb
i'll keep waiting to find something new

i'm hoping i can start to live through better days
i'll keep hoping that everything ends up okay
i hope that things calm down, hope one day i can say
i'm so happy that i'm here with you

i'm me again
07/20/2022

i'm transparent, slightly pink tinted, you're the deepest shade of red
when i tried to see myself i just saw through, saw you instead
i can't be a shadow of you, i don't cast shadows at all
and i could see myself again when i noticed that yours was gone

false image
07/21/2022

you are an angry shade of red and i'm the lightest shade of blue
you sliced me up and let me bleed to say i look just like you

user
07/26/2022

i understand that what i got from you was never truly love
you only "love" the people that you can make good use of
you love their effort, love their care, they way they always go above
you'll do nothing and soak it in until they're all used up
and then you're done, interest is gone, it's right onto the next one, or the last one, or the old one, one that still hasn't had enough
squeeze them dry, re-break their trust, decide again that you're done
then go back on the hunt to find the next one true love

harmonizing
08/05/2022

i allow my heartstrings to be played like a harp in a windowless basement
how familiar have you gotten with the tune of another? have you had to practice long?
i stay on the sideline of the orchestra of the street, i sit for a melody moving faster than headlights around turns
i stick around to find a tune that allows me to sing along

breaking a routine
08/08/2022

saying goodbye just for the sake of not trying until it breaks i let you take what you can take and then draw lines and walk away 'cause when i listen i get played by all the fake-kind things you say but i know all that shit is temporary, i know that it won't stay but all that's cool and it's okay cause i won't either anymore, i left the cycle on replay but i can't play that shit no more

good intentions
08/22/2022

i tried to hold your heart but in my hands it only bled because instead i had your pain, you let it bleed and turned me red

restart
08/31/2022

my scar tissue runs so deep it's stuck to the bone, i won't feel normal 'til i'm gone with the earth
i decompose the same way that i heal, all alone, and my thick skin takes me through my rebirth

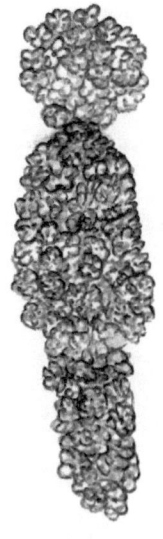

remembering, and that's all
10/05/2022

i'm sick of missing the past, wish i knew how to make things stay
i'm sick of knowing what i should've asked
sick of moving when there's more to say
knowing that hindsight is hindsight no matter how much you push it to change
but the efforts for nothing, the past is the past, it's behind me and now all of that's out of range

trust v. pattern
10/17/2022

how are they gonna feel when they hear your heart is breaking?
how are they gonna feel when they hear you think they're faking?
well if they are then they won't care-
and if they're not then it's not fair
yeah but i'm scared, it's in the air
i'm always wondering what's there
i'm sick of wondering what's there
i'm sick of wondering who's there
i'm sick of wondering who what when where
but why?
if it's that clear then why can i not see the signs?
am i just stupid, is it possible i'm blind?
i thought i figured all this out the last time that i had my doubts
but then the patterns in my mind, they tell me what it's all about
but you're a victim to yourself
there is nobody you're against
it's trust v pattern, get it right and break the cycle, let it rest

used
10/20/2022

they'll pretend that they care and they'll use you for sex then they'll throw you aside and treat you like the rest you're convinced of a friend & hold their love in your chest then it's torn out and stomped on and you're left abscessed it's a mess and i'm sick of taking all the tests and of trying my best because after it all i just lose the contest that i didn't sign up for like i'm on a quest like i always have to work to prove i'm the best but i can't be & won't be & i can't impress all the rest i'll always be a guest & i'll feel like a pest 'til i'm gone but until then i guess i'll repress all aspects of myself to navigate through this mess and get rid of the stress that i can and invest all my time in myself i'll hear what they suggest and i'll take a step back and then i'll reassess i won't be used for care i won't be used for sex and you pushed me aside as if you're like the rest i know i should've guessed that it wasn't the best to put my trust in you but the problems addressed and since i know what i should i'll take time to digest and assess the people that just get me undressed to relieve their own stress and even though i'm trying my best to get past all the falsehoods i still fight against facing lies of who cares 'cause i always forget people only talk to me when they have a request

destructive thoughts
10/31/2022

never the first picked, always the last
and my mental health feels like it's going down fast
i know i'm always stuck thinking, always hooked on the past
but how could i not be when i can't make things last
but the past is the past, yeah i know that by now
and the past gets messed up before i can see how
if i could watch the thoughts fly around and run them into the ground
and then burn it all down
then i would

love's downfall
11/11/2022

the honeymoon phase ends
rose tinted glasses lost their spark
the red flags just get brighter while the illusion falls apart
like a routine, day after day
stuck in a rut, stuck in decay
allow it all to just get worse until there's nothing left to say

stuck
11/11/2022

don't ask me how i'm doing 'cause im gonna have to lie to you
'cause telling you the truth on that's not something i'm able to do
i'm always dragged into this game, always involved in some odd way
i try to leave day after day but i end up here anyway
i'm forced to stay & play, to stick around and feed my own decay
i can't keep myself stuck in this state
i think i need to get away

losing
11/21/2022

i'm being left behind again
nothing to mend
i found a place with no dead end
i'm left alone in voids of space, think i ran out of time to spend
it all feels fake
and i can't shake it
now there's nothing left at stake
'cause now there's nothing left to face, and i don't even have a friend

come with me
12/01/2022

let me kiss your hand while i take you on a trip through the stars
let's drive off and be alone, let's go settle down on mars
with your hand in mine i know that i can make it far
so let me hang onto it tight and show you love isn't hard

now we really do look the same
12/01/2022

i'll rip the blood from my veins and cloak my body in the crimson
now i'm as red as you are, if we're even no one wins then

push it away
12/12/2022

i think i'm falling for you but i'll never let you know
because you'd turn around and tell me "now you need to let me go"
i been through this script, i've seen this scene, i've gone through this whole show
and the end's always the same, the girl is always 'fine alone'
but i don't wanna be your actor, and i don't wanna be your friend
i wanna be a bit more to you, can i hold your hand instead?
i guess i'll save that one for later, i won't cause another end
i'll keep it quiet, keep it shut, i'll keep the feeling good and dead

letting you go
12/21/2022

i think i stopped the world for you
while i held tightly to your hand
but now it's time to let it move
and let you fade off where i stand
my heart stays trapped inside a cage
with my head covered in the snow
but i noticed now the seasons change
and i can let the flowers grow

it's too different now
01/05/2023

we're not on the same wavelength anymore
hearing your day to day some days feels like a chore
because you used to be everything that i used to adore
and now you're turning into all the things you used to ignore

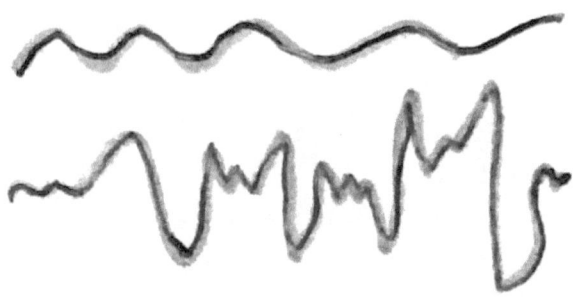

here for you
02/28/2023

we see the same moon, we see the same stars
we hold it together while we fall apart
you can bleed yourself on me and i'll hold your heart
you can lean yourself on me .'til you can restart
i've got your back and i'll be your backup
you can stay behind me, and i'll hold it at the front
i'll help you get through it 'til you feel less stuck
i know you'd do the same for me once you can get up
but take as long as you need, i'll stay by your side
know that you can trust me, know there's no need for you to hide
i'm here to do this with you, i'm not sure if i can guide
but if you let me in i'll stay along for the ride

to be winter
02/28/2023

the snow still tries to settle as the clock ticks towards morning
the flurries land and melt on the not quite cold enough asphalt, the lingering chill in the air hasn't done enough to keep the sheets alive
it comes as quickly as it goes
the sidewalk stays clear, the street stays dark
the sky is as beautiful as it is lonely
i know what it means to be winter

in need of a reset
03/02/2023

daydreaming of my death
bad thoughts always fill up my head
i wish i could go feel better but i can't get out of bed
they leave my messages on read
i think i'm relapsing again
when i'm spiraling sobriety is nothing but a test
i'm always left behind the rest
can't find what i should do instead
i try to help myself but i don't ever do what i intend
sometimes i think need a friend
maybe i need a full reset
to start anew without a clue and find a new and better end

remember me
03/06/2023

remember me as luck
remember me as loud
remember that to get it all i had to go without
remember me as drunk with love
remember me as proud
remember all the ways i had to move to stay around
remember me as stuck
remember me lost in the crowd
see me in the stars when you stop to look around
remember me as moonstruck
remember me below the ground
i'll be there when you look up & you see the sun and clouds

a short lived sight of beauty
03/07/2023

sheets of white cloak the city's streets as the clock hits a quiet 2AM
aside from the patter of flurries and the wave of a distant flag in the wind, it's quiet
the streets are clean and bright
the sky is black and white
the sight as lovely as it is temporary
these city streets will be busy by morning

low battery
04/07/2023

waking up and feeling insufficient
nothing different
try to get help & no one listens
i'm so damn sick of these conditions
it's all the same it's so reminiscent of the past
i play the game, i do the time, it doesn't last
i dedicate myself and it ends just as fast
my energy's about to crash
i'm about to run and cash out
i'm about to trip and pass out
everything is in the past now
i'm being left and passed again, i think i need to get the fuck out

all for you
04/30/2023

poem after poem
line after line
i dedicate to you my stanzas and rhymes
page after page
metaphors and similes
a book filled with examples of how i see you and me

wishing and wanting
05/07/2023

i long for peace of mind
to be ok with what i find
i long to feel alright
to not feel like i have to fight
i long to be embraced
to be with you, to share your space
i long to feel like i belong
to feel the same, to not feel wrong
i long to know who i should be
i long to be the best for me
i long to know where i should stay
i long for me to be okay

inside
05/07/2023

i'm floating through a space full of debris and devastation
i'm looking at what once has been okay
i'm flying through the mess and i can feel all the frustration
i'm staying somewhere that i shouldn't stay
my time inside this place has felt like all but a vacation
i feel i've gone from predator to prey
i've been fighting endlessly toward some sort of liberation
but i think that maybe i should go away

breaking the lines we dance between
05/13/2023

i want me to be yours and i want you to be mine
i think that would make all the things around me feel more fine
let me take your hand and baby we can tread the line between what's real and what's pretend, 'cause all of that is intertwined

the sound of stagnancy
05/19/2023

never have notifications
i check my phone but nothing's there
i think i need a small vacation
but i can't afford airfare
so i stay stuck in my hometown
but i sure need to find a change
i'm sick of just sticking around
for all these things to stay the same

About the author

Morgan was born in January 1998 in the southern area of Queens, NY. She's since lived down in Queens her whole life. She's been writing poetry as a hobby for fun since around 6th grade, and drawing even longer than that- for as long as she can remember. The trials of having a heart of empathy and the hardships of being a young adult in the modern world are two big things that fuel her latest works, as well as a clear up and down trip through the life of being a big lover in a world that doesn't want to reciprocate. She uses poetry and writing as a way to vent her struggles and worries while learning to deal with all that life has to offer, good and bad.

Somewhere between love and loss you can find the author sat on a bench writing about her thoughts through metaphors and rhymes. This collection is organized in chronological order and features poems from 2018-2023 following such themes as infatuation, isolation, betrayal, depression, and has glimpses into the inner monologue as well as an incessant pining for love. Follow through a rollercoaster featuring a loop of hope, a spray of angst and a grand ending of, well, usually heartache.

www.ingramcontent.com/pod-product-compliance
Lightning Source LLC
LaVergne TN
LVHW041631070526
838199LV00052B/3310